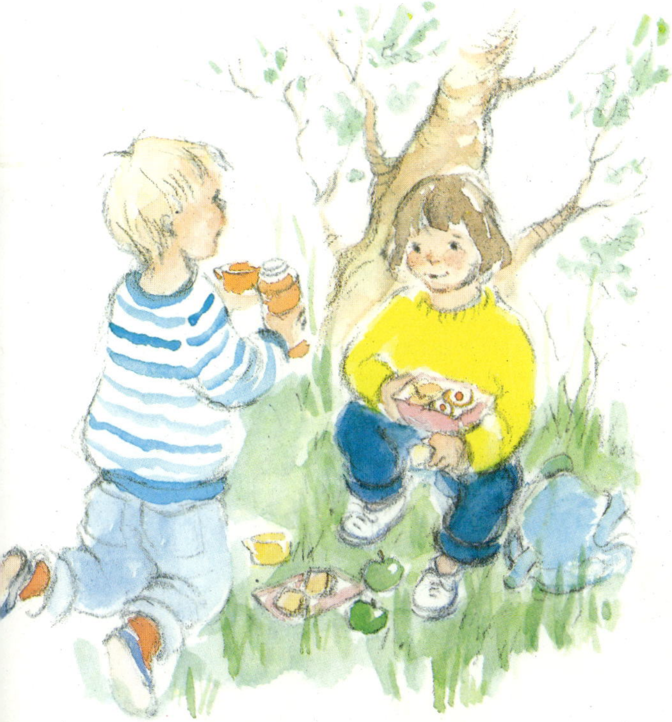

NOTE TO PARENTS

Songs For Jesus is a selection of songs praising Jesus which have been especially chosen with children in mind. The order of the songs follows the Christian year. Most of the songs are well-known, some traditional, some more modern, but all carry the message of the love that God has for everyone and everything.

Every effort has been made to trace the author and owner of the copyright of these songs. We offer our sincere apologies if we have used copyright material without due acknowledgement. *One more step*, *When I needed a neighbour* and *Think of a world* are reproduced by permission of Stainer and Bell Ltd. *He made me* copyright © 1970 by High-Fye Music Ltd., 8/9 Frith St., London W1. Used by permission. All rights reserved.

Songs For Jesus

selected by Marjorie Newman
illustrated by Dianne Stuchbury

Copyright © 1990 World International Publishing Limited.
All rights reserved.
Published in Great Britain by World International Publishing Limited,
An Egmont Company, Egmont House,
P.O. Box 111, Great Ducie Street,
Manchester M60 3BL.
Printed in DDR.
ISBN 0 7235 4469 7

A CIP catalogue record for this book is available from the British Library

Give Me Oil in My Lamp

Give me oil in my lamp, keep me burning.
Give me oil in my lamp, I pray.
Give me oil in my lamp, keep me burning,
Keep me burning till the break of day.

Sing Hosanna, sing Hosanna,
Sing Hosanna to the King of Kings!
Sing Hosanna, sing Hosanna,
Sing Hosanna to the King!

Give me joy in my heart, keep me singing.
Give me joy in my heart, I pray.
Give me joy in my heart, keep me singing,
Keep me singing till the break of day.

Give me love in my heart, keep me serving.
Give me love in my heart, I pray.
Give me love in my heart, keep me serving,
Keep me serving till the break of day.

Give me peace in my heart, keep me resting.
Give me peace in my heart, I pray.
Give me peace in my heart, keep me resting,
Keep me resting till the break of day.

Copyright control

JESUS BIDS US SHINE

Jesus bids us shine
With a pure, clear light,
Like a little candle
Burning in the night.
In this world of darkness,
So we must shine,
You in your small corner,
And I in mine.

Jesus bids us shine,
First of all for Him;
Well He sees and knows it,
If our light grows dim.
He looks down from Heaven
To see us shine,
You in your small corner,
And I in mine.

Jesus bids us shine,
Then for all around;
Many kinds of darkness
In this world are found.
Sin and want and sorrow,
So we must shine,
You in your small corner,
And I in mine.

Susan Warner 1819-1885

Kum Ba Yah

Kum ba yah, my Lord, Kum ba yah.
Kum ba yah, my Lord, Kum ba yah.
Kum ba yah, my Lord, Kum ba yah.
Oh Lord, Kum ba yah.

Someone's singing, Lord, Kum ba yah.
Someone's singing, Lord, Kum ba yah.
Someone's singing, Lord, Kum ba yah.
Oh Lord, Kum ba yah.

Someone's praying, Lord, Kum ba yah.
Someone's praying, Lord, Kum ba yah.
Someone's praying, Lord, Kum ba yah.
Oh Lord, Kum ba yah.

Someone's crying, Lord, Kum ba yah.
Someone's crying, Lord, Kum ba yah.
Someone's crying, Lord, Kum ba yah.
Oh Lord, Kum ba yah.

Someone's lonely, Lord, Kum ba yah.
Someone's lonely, Lord, Kum ba yah.
Someone's lonely, Lord, Kum ba yah.
Oh Lord, Kum ba yah.

Traditional

One More Step

One more step along the world I go,
One more step along the world I go,
From the old things to the new
Keep me travelling along with You.
And it's from the old I travel
  to the new.
Keep me travelling along with You.

Sydney Carter

When I Needed a Neighbour

When I needed a neighbour,
Were you there, were you there?
When I needed a neighbour,
Were you there?

*And the creed and the colour
And the name won't matter,
Were you there?*

I was hungry and thirsty,
Were you there, were you there?
I was hungry and thirsty,
Were you there?

I was cold, I was naked,
Were you there, were you there?
I was cold, I was naked,
Were you there?

When I needed a shelter
Were you there, were you there?
When I needed a shelter
Were you there?

When I needed a healer,
Were you there, were you there?
When I needed a healer,
Were you there?

Wherever you travel
I'll be there, I'll be there.
Wherever you travel
I'll be there.

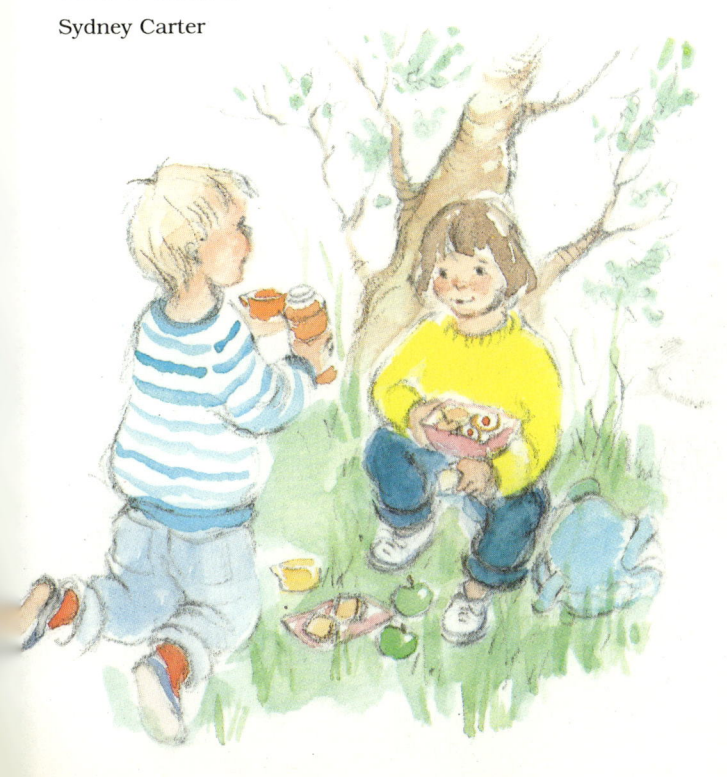

Sydney Carter

Tell Me the Stories of Jesus

Tell me the stories of Jesus
I love to hear.
Things I would ask Him to tell me
If He were here.
Scenes by the wayside,
Tales of the sea,
Stories of Jesus, tell them to me.

First let me hear how the children
Stood round His knee,
And I shall fancy His blessing
Resting on me.
Words full of kindness,
Deeds full of grace,
All in the lovelight of Jesus' face.

Into the city I'd follow
The children's band,
Waving a branch of a palm tree
High in my hand.
One of His heralds,
Yes I would sing
Loudest Hosannas! Jesus is King.

William Henry Parker 1845-1929

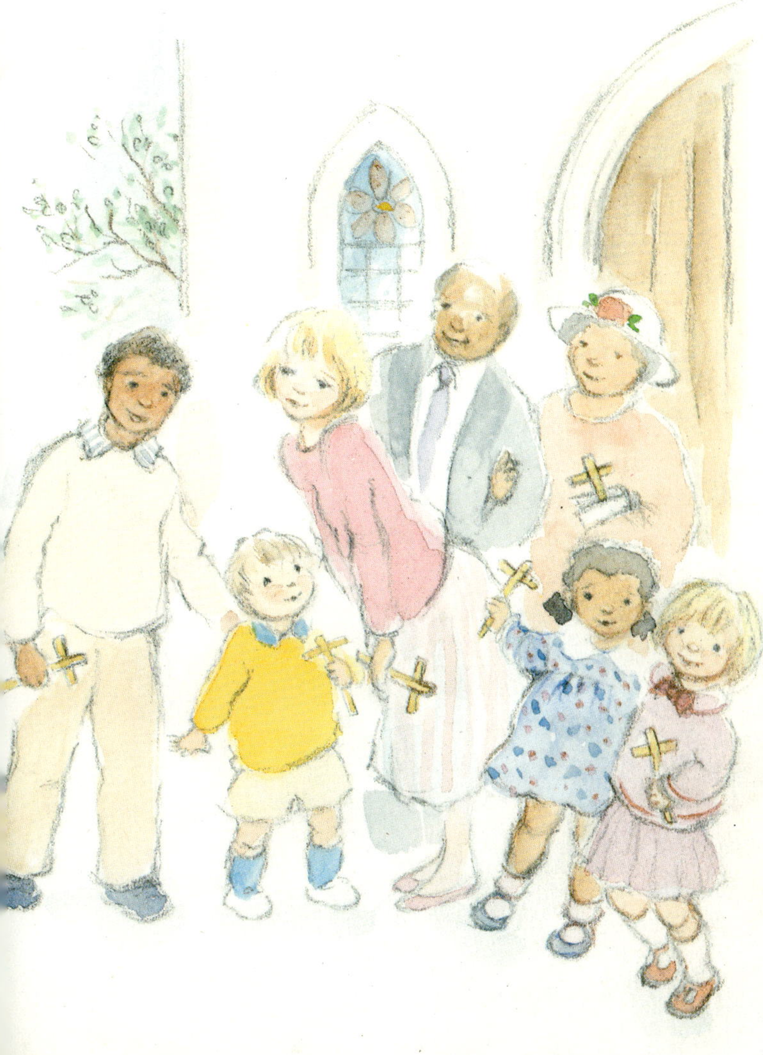

Praise Him, Praise Him

Praise Him, praise Him,
All you little children,
God is love, God is love.
Praise Him, praise Him,
All you little children,
God is love, God is love.

Love Him, love Him,
All you little children,
God is love, God is love.
Love Him, love Him,
All you little children,
God is love, God is love.

Thank Him, thank Him,
All you little children,
God is love, God is love.
Thank Him, thank Him,
All you little children,
God is love, God is love.

Traditional

This is the Day

This is the day, this is the day
That the Lord hath made,
That the Lord hath made.
I will rejoice, I will rejoice
And be glad in it, and be glad in it.
This is the day, this is the day
That the Lord hath made.

Copyright control

ALL THINGS BRIGHT AND BEAUTIFUL

All things bright and beautiful,
All creatures great and small,
All things wise and wonderful,
The Lord God made them all.

Each little flower that opens,
Each little bird that sings,
He made their glowing colours,
He made their tiny wings.

The purple-headed mountain,
The river running by,
The sunset, and the morning
That brightens up the sky.

The cold wind in the winter,
The pleasant summer sun,
The ripe fruits in the garden,
He made them, every one.

The tall trees in the greenwood,
The meadows where we play,
The rushes by the water
We gather every day.

He gave us eyes to see them
And lips that we might tell
How great is God almighty
Who has made all things well.

Cecil Frances Alexander, 1818-1895

He's Got the Whole World

He's got the whole world
In His hands,
He's got the whole wide world
In His hands,
He's got the whole world in His hands,
He's got the whole world in His hands.

He's got the wind and the rain
In His hands,
He's got the wind and the rain
In His hands,
He's got the wind and the rain
In His hands,
He's got the whole world in His hands.

He's got the sun and the moon
In His hands,
He's got the sun and the moon
In His hands,
He's got the sun and the moon
In His hands,
He's got the whole world in His hands.

He's got everybody here in His hands,
He's got everybody here in His hands,
He's got everybody here in His hands,
He's got the whole world in His hands.

Traditional

We Plough the Fields and Scatter

We plough the fields and scatter
The good seed on the land,
But it is fed and watered
By God's almighty hand:
He sends the snow in winter,
The warmth to swell the grain,
The breezes and the sunshine,
And soft refreshing rain.

All good gifts around us
Are sent from Heaven above;
Then thank the Lord, O thank the Lord,
For all His love.

He only is the maker
Of all things near and far,
He paints the wayside flower,
He lights the evening star.
The winds and waves obey Him,
By Him the birds are fed;
Much more to us, His children,
He gives our daily bread.

We thank Thee then, O Father,
For all things bright and good;
The seed-time and the harvest,
Our life, our health, our food.
No gifts have we to offer
For all Thy love imparts,
But that which Thou desirest,
Our humble, thankful hearts.

Matthias Claudius 1740-1815
(translated by Jane Montgomery Campbell 1817-1878)

He Made Me

He gave me eyes so I could see
The wonders of the world.
Without my eyes I could not see
The other boys and girls.
He gave me ears so I could hear
The wind and rain and sea.
I've got to tell it to the world,
He made me.

He gave me lips so I could speak
And say what's on my mind.
Without my lips I could not speak
A single word or line.
He made my mind so I could think,
And choose what I should be.
I've got to tell it to the world,
He made me.

He gave me hands so I could touch,
And hold a thousand things.
I need my hands to help me write,
To help me fetch and bring.
These feet He made so I could run,
He meant me to be free.
I've got to tell it to the world,
He made me.

Alan Pinnock

Think of a World Without Any Flowers

Think of a world without any flowers,
Think of a world without any trees,
Think of a sky without any sunshine,
Think of the air without any breeze.
We thank You, Lord,
For flowers and trees and sunshine.
We thank You, Lord,
And praise Your Holy Name.

Think of a world without any animals,
Think of a field without any herd,
Think of a stream without any fishes,
Think of a dawn without any bird.
We thank You, Lord,
For all Your living creatures.
We thank You, Lord,
And praise Your Holy Name.

Think of a world without any people,
Think of a street with no one living there,
Think of a town without any houses,
No one to love and nobody to care.
We thank You, Lord,
For families and friendships,
We thank You, Lord,
And praise Your Holy Name.

Doreen Newport

How Far is it to Bethlehem?

How far is it to Bethlehem?
Not very far.
Shall we find the stable room
Lit by a star?

Can we see the little Child?
Is He within?
If we lift the wooden latch,
May we go in?

May we stroke the creatures there,
Ox, ass or sheep?
May we peep like them, and see
Jesus asleep?

If we touch His tiny hand,
Will He awake?
Will He know we've come so far,
Just for His sake?

Frances Chesterton, (circa 1900)

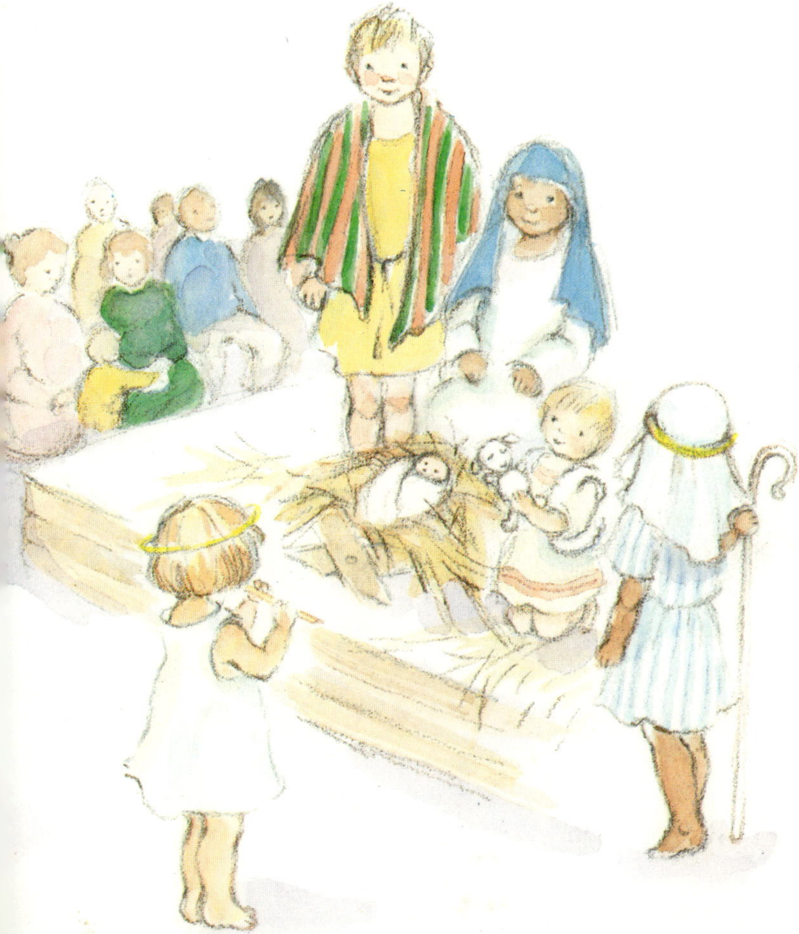